get some

Hairapy

A hairdresser's prescription
for happiness.

ISBN 0-7414-2773-7

Editing: Cara Francis, M.Ed.

Cover: Rita Lomas

Author's photo: Eustacia Mahoney

Published by:

PUBLISHING.COM

1094 New DeHaven Street, Suite 100
West Conshohocken, PA 19428-2713
Info@buybooksontheweb.com
www.buybooksontheweb.com
Toll-free (877) BUY BOOK
Local Phone (610) 941-9999
Fax (610) 941-9959

Printed in the United States of America

Printed on Recycled Paper

Published September 2005

Contents

Foreword

I remember my first "Beauty Shop" experience. I was seven years old and making my First Communion. This was a special occasion that warranted my maiden "beauty shop" visit. My mother and I walked half a block and across the street to a rather uninviting neighborhood establishment on the corner of First and Soto in Los Angeles. My mother wanted me to get a permanent; she thought it would be easier to manage. At that time, a permanent was a rather involved process. It began with the customary hair washing and then the application of rollers—mechanical devices used to curl hair—which were then attached to some bizarre apparatus. After several hours tied to this contraption, I was disconnected, rollers removed, my hair was rewashed and cut. I was transferred to the styling area, yet no styling was needed. I looked at my reflection and in the mirror and I saw a small brown child with an Afro. Either I was hipper than I thought--leading the Afro-centric craze of the late 60's--or I had my first bad hair experience.

Times have definitely changed. The term "beauty shop" has perished, although there are some neighbor-hood relics that remain. The term "Salons" has emerged. Today, salons are a big business. They offer a full scope of service that includes: facials, waxing, manicures, pedicures, hair products and make-up consultations.

But some things have not changed. Clients are still people, people still have problems they like to talk about, and hairdressers still hear about them.

Your hairdresser may not be a trained psychologist, but she may have some real world wisdom to hand out with your haircut. Listen up!

Christina M. Guillén-Cook, MBA, RN

What is Hairapy?

I tell my physician clients that I think I should be able to write prescriptions for certain mood altering medications. It seems fairly obvious to me who needs meds, who needs therapy, and who just needs to pull their head out of their ass.

They laugh and suggest that perhaps I should just refer those who I believe need help to the appropriate professionals. Ok. Fine. I can do that. I know plenty of psychiatrists, psychologists, family practice physicians and therapists.

But something needed to be done for the people who don't really need medicine or therapy. I wrote this book for them. Well, for us. This is a prescription for those of us who need to pull our heads out of our asses.

I have heard people say that bartenders hear everything, but let me tell you: Hairdressers hear more. We stand behind you, touching you, and for many people, that creates a feeling of safety that enables them to share the deepest, scariest parts of themselves and their lives.

Add to that the fact that hairdressers build relationships with clients that become more than just business. We are there through weddings, divorces, babies & tragedies. Our clients are a part of our lives. The salon is the center of my world. I met my husband through the salon, and I met my children (I adopted them when they were 4 and 6 years old) there as well. I have friends I can't imagine my life without who started as clients.

I never know what new adventure will walk though the front door and into my life.

I have as many issues as anybody.

I feel compelled to share this philosophy with you, not because my life is perfect and without hurdles (far from it!) but because I have these hurdles. I have been a wreck and I have been happy. Happy is better.

Here is a list of some of my issues (so you know I am not some Pollyanna who doesn't understand that life can be rough):

I have a brother who doesn't speak to me. I have stopped wondering why and just accept any contact he sends my way with love and grace. This year I got a birthday email from him that said, "OK, happy f***ing birthday." I imagine that this email followed a conversation with his wife, our mother, or our brother that went something like this: "Oh for crying out loud, can't you just wish your sister a happy f***ing birthday?" I graciously replied to his email, "Thank you!"

I have a 15 year old son who, one hour after leaving a 30 day lock-down drug treatment

3

program (after being arrested on a bench warrant issued by his probation officer) ran away. Again.

I have a mouthy 14 year old daughter who knows everything and thinks I am an idiot.

I was once a mouthy 14 year old who knew everything and thought my mother was an idiot. (She's gotten a lot smarter since then.)

I have been divorced.

I have been depressed & medicated.

I have been depressed and self-medicated!

I have been to therapy.

Today I choose to be happy. You can, too.

You are responsible for your own happiness.

People ask me how I can keep it together when things go wrong; especially when it comes to my son. I have given this a great deal of thought, because it comes up a lot.

The first question is "How can you be so calm when your son is a runaway and you don't know where he is or if he is OK?" That question is often followed by the statement, "If it were me, I would be freaking out!"

Let's dissect this.

First is the question: how can I be calm?

Well, I tried freaking out, and I tried crying myself to sleep, and I tried staring at the wall in a semi-catatonic state of depression. None of those approaches made the situation any better. In fact, the only thing they did was take a physical, emotional and spiritual toll on me.

Second is the statement: if it were me....

I had to get over the guilt I felt for choosing to be happy, even though things were crappy. I felt that I was being judged. I felt that people were thinking that if I were a good mother I would be freaking out and that any other response meant that I was inadequate, uncaring and wrong.

I have read a lot of books written by survivors of tragedy, and the one thing I can tell you they all say is that at some point, you have to make a choice to go on with your life.

If you spend all your time dwelling on things over which you have no control, you miss out on the things you can control. If you get nothing else from this book, get this. Every human being deserves happiness. You choose it. You choose your mood and your outlook. Things can be bumpy in your life and you can still choose to be happy!

Life is a smorgasbord. There is a big, long table full of choices, and there's just not room for all of them on your plate. Are you going to fill up your plate with misery or are you going to choose happiness (and maybe some pie)?

Stop shooting yourself in the foot and then wondering why your foot hurts!

Maybe you don't want to be happy. Perhaps you are under the impression that being miserable is OK. The problem with that is that no one wants to be around miserable people!

If you really want to be miserable; go isolate yourself in a cabin in the woods like the Unibomber. I promise we won't come looking for you and we won't miss you.

The definition of insanity is doing the same thing over and over and expecting a different result.

If you want to change your life, you have to change your outlook and change your actions.

Are you willing to try?

Do you want to be right or do you want to be happy?

I spent most of my life worrying about convincing people how right I was. Maybe it's because I am the first born child, maybe it's because my parents are brilliant and I wanted them to see that I was, also. Who knows?

I once had a fight with my first husband over the definitions and difference between the words "chore" and "errand."

He believed them to be synonymous, and I saw them as distinctly different. An errand is something you run, therefore implying leaving where you are and going somewhere else. A chore is an unpleasant task, usually used to describe something you do where you are.

Can you imagine? What kind of person has an actual fight over something so silly?

But I was right and I held on to that like a pit bull. I even went to the effort of purchasing a new dictionary to prove that I was right. Being right somehow seemed the same as being good, in fact I was convinced that the only thing better than being good is being better than someone (or everyone) else.

In school, I used to have to be the first to turn in a test. If I wasn't first, how would everyone know that I was smart (and therefore worthy)? One day I drove past a billboard that said "Do you want to be right or do you want to be happy?"

Wasn't it nice of those people to put up a sign just for me? How did they know that was exactly the way to put it so that I would (finally) get it?

Let me tell you, being happy is way better than being right.

If being right is the only thing that makes you happy, then life will find a way to make you right.

Think your spouse will cheat on you? Think you're going to lose your job? Think it enough and it will happen. It's called a self-fulfilling prophesy and I know you have seen it happen!

Still want to be right?

Pleasure is not happiness.

Pleasure is not bad. The only thing wrong with pleasure is that it can distract you from your true happiness.

The Dalai Lama wrote that the purpose of life is to seek happiness, but that human beings have a tough time distinguishing between happiness and pleasure.

Will buying another purse make me happy? I have plenty of purses. I have a giant Rubbermaid storage bin full of purses. My kids call me a Bag Lady. Buying a purse brings me pleasure. I like the feel of great leather, I like to have pretty things, and I like the attention I get from people commenting on my new bag.

But a new purse won't make me happy.

Want a facelift? Have one.

Think it will make you happy? Think again.

Look at Michael Jackson. Perhaps he should have spent some of his money on therapy instead of surgery. Do you think he is happy?

This is the lesson I am trying to teach my son. Getting high and living by your own rules may be pleasant, but I truly believe it is not the road to true happiness. I just have to convince him. (Ever had any luck convincing a 15 year old of anything?)

It's hard to be happy when you are a victim.

Here is a powerful fact of life: Crappy things happen to everyone! You do not hold the exclusive rights to this.

There are those who believe that you create everything that happens to you. You can believe that or not. But there is one thing you can not deny:

You do have control over how you react to the crappy things that happen to you.

What writes the story of your life is not what happens to you, but how you handle it.

Would you like people to think of you as a victim of adversity or as someone who overcame adversity?

If you ever start feeling sorry for yourself (an incredibly unattractive habit, I assure you) remember this:

I was sad that I had no shoes until I met a man who had no feet.

There will always be someone with a sadder story than yours.

As Dolly Parton once said, "Get off the cross. Someone needs the wood!"

No one keeps you a victim without your permission.

I knew a woman who had an inappropriate relationship with a female teacher when she was in middle school. The reason I knew this about her was because it was the reason she gave for why everything in her life was a mess.

If you asked her why she couldn't be a responsible grown-up, she would tell you it was because of this bad thing that happened to her. She had given herself permission to be a failure her entire life because of one thing that happened when she was a kid. And her parents, who felt sorry for her, and guilty for not protecting her from it, continue to aid and abet this idea by rescuing and protecting her from everything they can.

I saw a headline over a clients shoulder yesterday that said, "It's never too late to have an OK childhood." I didn't read the article, but I assume it went something like this: change the way you think about your past and it will change your future.

Does whining and carrying on about how bad things used to be make one bit of difference? Does it change what happened?

The past is the past. Get over it.

I had a therapist who wanted to talk about whom to blame for why I was depressed. Did a parent not love me enough? Was someone emotionally unavailable? I told her that the people in my past did the best with what they had and that I wasn't interested in blaming, just changing myself.

I found a different therapist.

Find something to be grateful for.

This morning one of my dogs woke me up at 3:45AM! Boy was I mad! I don't like to be awake at 3:45 AM. I like to sleep. I am good at it. My husband hates that I can be asleep within moments of closing my eyes. So there I was, 3:45 AM, irritated and wide awake.

And I started thinking about all the ways my dogs give me trouble. Damn beasts! Why did I have them anyway?

Well, I got a dog after my divorce for companionship and a little unconditional love.

I went online and took quizzes to select the right breed of dog. I read dog books. I knew I wanted a full-size dog. I knew that I wanted one that required little grooming because I do enough hair at work, thank you very much.

I chose a Great Dane with the full knowledge that it would want to hang out on the couch with the family and may even be labeled lazy which works out great, since some people would label me lazy.

If you have never seen a Great Dane puppy, you have no idea how adorable an 18 pound, 10 week old can be. I named him Texas (because he was going to be big and because I had a bumper sticker I was going to put on the fence that said Don't Mess With Texas) and he slept in a laundry basket beside my bed.

After a few weeks, I started to feel guilty about leaving him alone while I was at work. So, in a moment of absolute insanity, I went back to the breeder and got his sister and named her Georgia.

What I learned is that puppies (like children) get into more trouble and are more difficult when there is more than one of them. They cook up trouble. They eat shoes and furniture and even drywall. (The dogs, not the children!)

One day they almost ate Ginger.

Ginger is the tiny white Toto-look-alike who, up until she met Texas & Georgia, enjoyed taking long walks with her owner. I had seen them in the neighborhood for years. Their regular walks took them past the window of my salon.

One day when my monsters were 10 months old and roughly 100 pounds a piece, I brought them to work to show a client how they had grown. After the visit with the client (a dog lover with a Newfoundland, a hound even bigger than a Dane) I grabbed both their leashes, wound them around my hand, and began to walk back to my car from the storefront.

Suddenly, they spotted the unsuspecting Ginger out for her afternoon stroll.

Before I knew what was happening, the beasts had pulled the leashes from my hand, making a hideous gash across three fingers as the nylon leash burned its way out of my grip. (I bought leather leashes after that. They don't slice and burn.)

They cornered Ginger, snarling and barking and frightening the poor thing so that she broke loose of her leash and headed, full-speed, across they busy afternoon traffic of the main street.

Thankfully, when the prey (or territorial inter-loper) was out of their immediate sight, the big dumb dogs allowed themselves to be corralled by the client, myself, and the staff who had rushed out when they heard all hell breaking loose outside the window.

Wounded hand throbbing, I regained leash control and secured them in the car.

The evil brutes, showing no signs of remorse, and I drove off to help find Ginger who was, by now, more than 5 blocks away from where the big mean dogs had scared her half to death. She was cowering in a flowerbed; her aged, shaken owner trying to soothe her while catching her own breath.

I arrived in time to hear Ginger's Mom telling the woman (whose flowers were being crushed by the terrified terrier) how two huge mean black dogs attacked her baby.

For the record, we had been to puppy obedience class. They were shameful there, as well. At our last class, Texas was sent to the corner with a chew toy to keep him from trying to eat his classmates.

I lay in bed at 4AM and thought about this incident and then I got to thinking philosophically. I could choose to dwell on the bad things, or I could choose to be grateful.

I am grateful I have my dogs. I sleep safe knowing that no intruder will cause me harm while they are with me. I am grateful that Texas woke me rather than toileting in the house (you can imagine how happy I would have been to clean up a Great Dane sized pile or puddle!) I am grateful that I have a cozy bed. I am grateful for my home and my family. I have a pretty good life.

I changed my thoughts from anger and blame to gratefulness. And I got out of bed and came to the computer and started writing about happiness!

Not too shabby.

It doesn't cost you anything to be nice.

My daughter is one of the beautiful people. I say this without the normal braggadocio you expect to hear from a parent: "My child is brilliant!" "My child is beautiful!"

It's not that. I may be the least "braggy" person you'll meet. I know that my children have flaws. It is my job to try to help them overcome them before I have to kill them for being so wretched.

Being beautiful isn't a flaw, but being rude is.

When people meet her for the first (and sometimes the second or third time) they comment on how beautiful her eyes are. She has become so used to hearing it, that she has ceased to see it as a compliment and does not graciously accept it with thanks.

It goes something like this:

Me: I'd like you to meet my daughter.

Stranger:	Nice to meet you! My, what beautiful eyes you have!
Daughter:	(rolls eyes) Um hmm.
Stranger:	(embarrassed, smiles) You must hear that all the time.
Daughter:	Yeah.

So the last time this happened I decided it was time for me to try to teach my daughter to be gracious. Beauty may leave you, but you can always choose to be kind.

We had it out in the parking lot of the mall. I told her that the proper response to a compliment is to smile and say "Thank you!" She expressed that this might be difficult for her. I told her that when someone compliments her, she should act like it's the first time she's ever heard it. Just smile and say "Thank you!" It doesn't seem that hard.

I used to have trouble accepting compliments, but for a different reason.

If you told me, "Wow, you look really great today!" What I heard was, "As opposed to every other day, when you look like hell." When I realized that I had a problem with that, I worked on it. Now when someone tells me I look nice, I smile and say "Thank you!" And I might even add, "That's so sweet of you to say!"

I have often had to train this child to "act" in social situations. What comes to mind is not always the most appropriate remark.

When she was five and was getting fitted for ballet shoes, the sales girl (who was also my client) knelt down to measure her feet. My daughter looked at the top of the sales girl's head and said "You need your hair color done." The client, embarrassed, muttered, "I have an appointment next week."

At age seven, we popped in to visit her grandparents. Her grandfather, a retired CEO (used to his requests being unquestioningly carried out), told her not to go upstairs.

Grandfather: I don't want you to go upstairs.

Child: Why?

Grandfather: Because I asked you not to.

Child: Why?

Grandfather: Because I asked you not to and because it's my house.

Child: No it's not. It's Grandma's house.

I thought he was going to kill her.

I could read his mind and knew what he was thinking. "This is my house. I paid for it. I pay the taxes. I worked my whole life for this family and I get back-talk from my own grandchild? I would have never spoken that way to my Grand-parents. Damn kids, these days. And what's wrong with her parents? Don't they teach her to respect her elders?"

His face was purple. He showed great restraint and did not kill her. Instead he hollered "Just don't go upstairs!" and walked away.

Later, when I had her alone, I told her that the proper way to respond when her grandfather asks her to do something is to say, "Ok, Grandpa."

How do you define yourself?

One woman introduced herself to me on her first visit to the salon and within 30 seconds had told me that she had been divorced many times. She even said the exact number of times; as in "Hello, my name is Martha. I need my color done and I have been divorced 5 times."

I told her I found it odd that she felt the need to share that with me.

On the next visit she told me that she had talked to her therapist about our conversation and that she had come now to a turning point in her life.

She didn't owe anyone an explanation of her past, and she didn't need to define herself as The Woman with Many Failed Marriages.

I am happy to say that she is currently in a relationship that she hardly recognizes because it is healthy. Go figure.

Even someone with a rocky track record can make the choice to have happiness.

Damaged people attract damaged people.

Want to meet someone stable, calm and successful?

Be someone stable, calm and successful.

If you are always drawn to people who are a wreck, you must have some wreckage of your own to clear up.

This is not news to you. You know this because you can see it in other people. Every one of us has a friend who is screwed up and keeps picking screwed up people to date and (God forbid) marry.

Don't be one of those people!

If you have issues of your own, work them out before you drag someone else into your nightmare. It's hard to work on a relationship and work on yourself. Focus on you, then when you feel like you have your head screwed on straight, you can look for an equally with-it, together partner.

Why would a with-it, together person want to date someone whose life is a train wreck?

And why would you want to date someone who was attracted to train wrecks?

You can coach, cajole and encourage, but you can't make anyone else happy. They have to do it themselves.

When my children were very small we sought therapy because my son was hitting his sister. The therapist asked him why he was hitting his sister. He said that she made him hit her. The therapist acted excited and said, "Wow! She has magical powers? She can sit over there and make you hit her! Wow!"

You can see how silly that is.

It is no sillier to think that you can make someone happy.

Their life = their choice.

The only thing about others that you can control is how you respond to them.

I have found it easier to hang out with happy people than to try to make cranky people happy.

Maybe I'm just getting lazy in my old age.

Be careful what you wish for, you just might get it.

A friend of mine recently learned this hard lesson.

She was feeling sorry for herself because she was single and lonely. (BTW, single and lonely are two different states of being. You can easily be one without being the other. I know single people who are not lonely and I know lonely people in relationships. I bet you do, too.)

During her pity party, she watched Wuthering Heights. She wished that she could have someone in her life who loved her as much as Heathcliff loved Cathy. "Where is my Heathcliff?" she wailed while she watched the movie a few more times.

Days later she saw a handsome, brooding man in her neighborhood. She turned to her friend and announced, "There's my Heathcliff!"

Shortly after, she told me she had a boyfriend, that the chemistry was amazing, and that he was "a project".

A little jail time, a little drug history, you know, lots of fun!

A year or two later, when he could no longer reign in his bad boy ways and she had to ask him to move out, he got a little crazy and she got a little scared.

How could this person who loved her so much be so frightening?

Guess she got what she wished for.

She thinks she has learned a thing or two from this and when wishing for love next time, she will pick a different movie!

Don't be a rescuer!

People need to fix themselves; they don't need you to do it for them. It won't work anyway. I've tried. We've all tried. If you meet someone who needs a therapist or social worker, get them one.

Whatever you do, don't date them! And for God's sake, don't marry them.

I met my current husband while I was shopping for a new best guy friend. I had recently lost my best guy friend because he had a new girlfriend.

It seemed crazy to me that a girlfriend should keep you from hanging out with your friends, but apparently there are women like that. If you are one of those women, KNOCK IT OFF! You either trust your partner or you don't. If you don't trust him, don't date him.

This woman would only allow her man to have friends who happened to have penises. Since I didn't have one, I was out. She wouldn't even let him come to the salon for haircuts, for crying out loud!

But he LOVED her! (Insert eye rolling here.)

What I really think he loved was her neediness. She was a recently divorced, single mother of two with no job skills. He, a big, strong man, was going to be her knight in shining armor. In exchange, she would fulfill his every fantasy. So if she wanted him to "break up" with me, he would.

I was devastated. I tried to explain to him how hurt I was, but he didn't seem to get it.

Through mutual friends I heard about the drama as it unfolded. They were engaged, they were moving in together, and she became stranger and stranger.

At his best friend's wedding, she became intoxicated.

Now, I can't say that I have never been intoxicated in public. And I can't say that I never embarrassed myself or others.

But I can say that I have never grabbed the crotch of the father of the bride.

As you can imagine, this caused quite the uproar.

The bride was mortified and didn't want to see the woman again, and so that caused trouble between the two men who had been best friends since college.

Eventually my former friend ended that relationship.

Perhaps he realized that he couldn't rescue her from her demons, perhaps he grew tired of the drama.

He's back at the salon these days. He just bought a house and married a woman who I hear is sane and reasonable. He has patched his friendship with his college buddy.

He and I will never be the same because we aren't in the same place in our lives as we were then. But we are OK. We can have a beer and laugh about the past.

And I did meet my husband because of all this drama, so I have to believe that good can come of bad.

You allow bad relationships to continue.

Change them or leave them.

OK, well maybe that's a little harsh. I am not so callous as to say that you should dispose of everyone in your life that won't go along with your plan.

You first have to give them a chance to join you in your happiness.

Toward the end of my first marriage, I became consumed with the desire to go to Italy. I wanted my husband and me to travel together. I thought it might be good for our floundering relationship to have an adventure together.

I brought it up many times and the answer was always No. There were many reasons why, but I had a rebuttal or solution to all of them. This was something that had become very important to me.

One day in the car (a great place to have discussions because you don't have to look at the other person) I said, "I am going to Italy. You can come or not. I don't care."

You can imagine how that went over.

The day my divorce was final I was on a plane to Rome.

I had given him the opportunity to come along on my journey (literal and figurative) and he chose not to.

Some people can't or won't choose happiness. You can be upset with them, or you can feel sympathy for them. It is pretty sad to think that someone just can't get out of their own way long enough to experience a little joy.

After an episode of Oprah about Toxic Friends, my co-worker divested herself of all the people who just would not stop sucking the life from her. I missed that episode, but boy howdy, that's something I can get behind!

If you have someone in your life sucking energy, it's pretty hard to keep up the energy for the things that don't suck.

Remember the story about the pitcher? If you are a pitcher, and all day long you fill up everyone else's glasses, eventually you will be empty. If you want to continue to give to others, you have to fill up the pitcher!

Sometimes you have to be selfish!

That might be something that your mother never told you, but it is true.

My son has a habit of running away. Since he thinks that he should be able to come and go as he pleases, it makes sense (to him) to camp out, commune-style, with other lost souls. They sleep in garages of friends, in abandoned houses, and occasionally outside.

You can imagine how difficult this is for me as a mother.

When he would call and say he wanted to come home, I would be so relieved that I would let him come home, never knowing if he meant for a day or to stay. Often it would be just long enough to shower, change clothes, have a good meal and a good nap.

The last time he was gone, he called and asked if he could come home to take a shower. I said no. I told him that our home was not a hotel and that to receive the benefits of community and family, he had to accept the responsibilities as well. I told him to call me when he was ready to stand up and take responsibility for his actions.

I'm not saying it wasn't hard. It was. But I was out of ideas of how to help him, and was driving myself nuts worrying about him. For my own mental health, I had to draw a line.

I also had to let go of any guilt associated with my decision. I had to accept that I had done everything within my power to help this kid, and now it was his time to choose.

I have a client who does not speak to her adult son.

It is so hard to imagine.

But I know this woman pretty well, and I know her to be caring and wise. If she had to make the incredibly difficult decision to do this, there must be reason.

Her son continues to see the world through a filter of "What's in it for me?" He has even defrauded his aged grandparents of their savings. I've got to say; there is something really wrong about stealing from your grandparents.

When I talked about this with my ex-husband, he wondered why I thought stealing from your grandparents was worse than stealing from your parents. I told him that your grandparents love you differently than your parents do.

They don't have the same daily struggles with you and they don't expect you to screw them! Your parent might have an idea that you can't be trusted, but your grandparents still believe in you!

What kind of a jackass steals from the only people who believe in him?

Hell, I wouldn't talk to him, either!

Sometimes you have to compromise.

You can't be selfish all the time! It's all about balance. Sometimes you give, and sometimes you take. There is nothing wrong with being forceful and assertive. After all, somebody has to get things done.

You just need to make sure that you don't behave like a bulldozer, pushing over other people and their feelings in your rush to get things done.

My husband understands this.

We bought a new house last year. The kitchen walls were a really wimpy, watery yellow, with one baby blue accent wall. There was no way in hell I was going to be happy with that. I tested out several paint shades and finally decided on a bright marigold with an accent wall of tomato soup red. It has a kind of Spanish country feel. My son HATES it!

One day when he was griping about it, my husband tried to give him some wisdom and insight.

Now, for the record, my husband thinks beige is a perfectly acceptable wall color. I, on the other hand, think that beige is not a color choice; it's a cry for help.

He said to the boy, "Just let it go. You see, when we let your mother do things she wants to do, then she lets us do things we want to do. Do you really want to fight over the color of your mother's kitchen? Think, man, think!"

I think this is one of the most brilliant things a young man can learn about dealing with women, and it's not a bad lesson for the rest of us, either! If you give a little, now and again, then others are more likely to give in when you want something.

No one likes a martyr.

I have always done things (because it was the right thing to do) for others, but when I was a miserable, depressed wreck, I resented it. I felt oppressed. I would do it, but I would sigh deeply and feel like a martyr.

Now that I am a happier person, I don't mind doing something nice for the people in my life. Part of it is feeling balanced on the inside and part of it is feeling appreciated on the outside.

It's easier to get excited about preparing meals for your family when they are grateful and make an effort to express that gratitude. (Some family members might need you to tell them that their gratitude should be expressed!)

I also feel better about having boundaries and saying no.

A friend sent me an online invitation to her jewelry party. I replied that I would not attend. She called and tried to talk me into coming.

Friend: Why aren't you coming?

Me:	I have to do a bride's hair early the following morning.
Friend:	Why don't you just come by for a while?
Me:	I have enough costume jewelry.
Friend:	Why don't you just come by for a few dinks?
Me:	I don't like those parties and I don't want to come!
Friend:	OK, then!

I could have handled it better by saying, "I prefer to come over and visit when there are fewer people there. Can we pick a time to BBQ with our families?" Lucky for me her feelings weren't hurt too badly and we are still friends.

No whining!

When someone asks how you are, they aren't looking for a laundry list of complaints.

During turbulent times with my son, it is sometimes hard to answer "How are you?"

I found that an honest, but not whiny, response we all could deal with was: "I've been better and I've been worse, but I'm OK."

Recently we had a client whose teenage son died from a sudden illness. When she came in for her first visit after his death, we asked her how she was doing. She said: "I'm breathing and I'm standing up." Sometimes that's all you can ask for.

Are you spending all your energy complaining that life isn't fair?

Didn't your mother tell you that life isn't fair?

Get used to it.

Sometimes you will not get what you feel you deserve.

Sometimes parents treat one child better than others.

Sometimes you get a speeding ticket that you think is unreasonable.

Sometimes someone else will get the promotion you had your heart set on.

Deal with it. Overcome. Adapt. Let it go!

Remember in *Moonstruck* when Nicholas Cage tells Cher he is in love with her? She smacks him on the head and tells him, "Snap out of it!"

Don't you wish you could do that to some people?

You choose who you allow into your life.

When my salon first opened, we were desperate for clients.

New businesses are like new babies; you worry about them and watch them constantly, hoping they will grow and thrive.

I had some existing clients from my years working in the business, but I also had hired some staff and they needed clients. We needed revenue if we were going to make it!

We walked the neighborhood and put out flyers and doorknob hangers.

We introduced ourselves to the neighboring businesses.

We wanted any client with hair and money, and we wanted their friends and their grandmother, and their housekeeper!

And we grew. We added more staff. One day, I found I was signing 14 paychecks. We were thriving.

But the staff meetings weren't going well. We were constantly complaining about the same things.

Stylist A is too loud; the clients don't want to hear about Stylist B's bar hopping and hangover; Stylist C's clients are all from the same church and they feel uncomfortable because Stylist D uses graphic language.

You get the point.

We were trying to attract every client, but we couldn't please every one of them. It was time to do some serious soul searching. If a business has a personality, we had a personality disorder!

Economically, the world was changing at the same time. The "middle" of our industry was disappearing. The chain salons (Regis, etc) had laid claim to that segment of the market and were really doing well with it.

The lower end of the market was pretty full, too, with places like SuperCuts. As a small, independent salon, we had to choose a path, and given our location near an affluent neighborhood, we chose to seek the higher end of the market.

Well, that thinned out our client list some. It also thinned out our staff. I remember one stylist who said she didn't want to have clients who could afford our new prices. She equated affluence with assholeness. (I found that interesting. I wasn't raised to believe that if you could afford nice things that you were automatically a jerk. That stylist later married an affluent man. I'll have to ask her if that changed her outlook.)

So now we were a more manageable size, but something still wasn't right. Now that we were charging higher prices the belief of the staff was that we needed to be "more professional." So we dressed nicer, turned down the music, and turned down our personalities.

It almost killed us (emotionally and financially.)

We found ourselves at another crossroads. We were not turning first time visitors into long term clients. I didn't understand. We did great work. What was missing?

One day I was sitting on a plane next to a man reading a book from the Harvard Business Press. It was called the Experience Economy. The first paragraph changed the way I looked at my business.

It said: What would you do differently tomorrow if instead of charging for your goods and services, you charged admission?

Clearly, my salon wasn't worth the price of admission!

We needed to find out who we were and what we had to offer. We knew we did good work and used good products, so it was obviously something intangible. What would set us apart from the other "nice" salons in our town?

I went back to all the nagging staff meetings and realized that what we had been complaining about was actually the one thing that could save us!

We would be the "fun" salon. We would let the staff chatter and encourage the clients to interact with each other. We would be the casual place where people like us (interesting, funny, often sarcastic) could be comfortable. And we gave ourselves permission to be successful.

And it worked! We were named to a "Best of" list in Seattle. Clients came and stayed. They sent in friends and family who would "get" us. Now our clients warn the customers they send in. "It's a little crazy there, but you'll love it. You can wear your pajamas and cuss."

Now we put a warning on our web site along with a message about how to choose a salon. (Read it here: www.azarra.com/howtochoose.htm)

We have reached a point where we are fortunate enough that we can be more selective about what clients we get, and that translates into more clients that we keep.

Now work is fun, AND we make a living! And it only took a decade of trying to be something we weren't to realize that we could be successful being ourselves.

I'm slow, but I catch on! I now teach a seminar to hairdressers called Getting and Keeping the Clients You Want!

The same thing goes for staff. This December, I got notice that a staff member would be leaving. I wanted to fill her spot, but I didn't want to get someone in who wasn't a good match. So I let go of the money concerns and had faith that the right person would come along.

I chatted up the network, and told all the beauty supply houses that we had a space available. I ran a classified ad, even though I haven't had a lot of success with them in the past. All this was in January.

As I write this, it is May and we have just added a new face to our business. He found us, but not through any of the channels I had set up. He came to us because he wants to become a Board Certified Haircolorist and really wanted to work with people who had accomplished that goal. He just started, but he seems just silly and smart-assed enough to fit in.

People can listen without hearing

While cleaning out the garage in preparation to move, I found opened bottles of lawn chemicals, spray paint, and whatnot. I asked my son if he had been "huffing" them.

He said no. He had been lighting them on fire!

Stunned, I asked him, "Didn't your mother tell you not to play with fire?!" He said, "She told me, I just didn't listen."

A friend of mine who works with adolescents defines that concept. "He's not listening" really means: He listened, he heard, he evaluated carefully what was said and he chose to blow off the adult who sadly thought they had control over his actions.

Every day I do not kill my son is a good day!

Or here's something that just makes me crazy. I have spent years training staff members; working with them daily on the finer points of color. Invariably when they return from a color class taught by someone else, they will be thrilled to tell me about the NEW thing they learned. More often than not, this new nugget of knowledge is something that I had said to them a thousand times. I speak; but they do not hear!

Your children have their own journey plan. You can contribute to it, but you can not control it.

My son has to learn everything the hard way. He is incredibly kind and likable, but he makes some of the stupidest choices you can imagine.

And he knows they are stupid choices!

I know this because the last time he ran away he left a note saying "I am sorry I make stupid choices that make you sad and piss you off."

Clearly this is not a stupid person!

You can boil down my son's issues to this core point: life is boring, getting high is fun, and even though he is 15 he should be able to come and go as he pleases.

And he seems perplexed that I have a problem with that.

My mother says that if I do kill my son, make sure I get a jury full of mothers of teenagers and they will acquit me.

She also suggests building a tower and locking him in it until he is 18.

Every day I do not kill my son is a good day!

Did you ever read *Lord of the Flies*? The whole time I was reading it I could only think of one thing.

Perhaps there could be an island where we could send all the teenagers. Then they wouldn't have to put up with us and we wouldn't have to put up with them. Whoever lived could come back when they were 18 and pleasant.

Teenagers are insane. I think they all are bi-polar. You never know which mood they will hit you with. They might be sweet and pleasant, but they are just softening you up for when the evil mood strikes and you begin to understand why some animals eat their young.

I am told they become human after they are old enough to move out.

When I was complaining to my mother once about how my daughter was driving me crazy, she laughed at me.

Laughed!

I was turning to her for advice, and she laughed at me.

I was perplexed. I honestly did not understand that I was a wretched child. I asked her, "At what age was I easiest to parent?"

Her response: "Adulthood."

Forgive the offender, forgive yourself.

When I was a young woman, I was raped.

This young man, a classmate, was so intoxicated, that his recollection of the events was faulty. He believed it was sort of consensual. He believed he had talked me into it. (That's a great coup for a boy in high school!) Word around the locker room was that he had sex with me, making no mention of how it came about.

I was angry.

I was ashamed.

I hated him and told the story from my perspective to anyone who would listen. I went on that way for more than a year. I would leave a room if he walked in. I spoke harshly of him if his name came up in conversation.

It was eating me alive. All I could think of was how much I hated him.

One day, I realized that hating him didn't hurt him at all, and it hurt me a lot.

And I let go. I forgave him. And I forgave myself for any part I had in the events of that night and for all the anger and hatred that came about after it.

And I felt better.

I felt lighter. When you hear people talk about a weight being lifted off their shoulders, it is real. You really feel lighter when you let down your burden.

Not long after that, he came into a room, and I didn't leave it. He sat beside me and in a few brief words, he apologized.

And because I had already forgiven him, I could graciously accept the apology.

My mother first heard this story when I sent her a first draft of this book to read. She asked me why I had not told her.

I told her that at the time I did not think that she would understand.

This reinforces my previously stated belief that teenagers are insane.

What's really going on?

My co-worker asked me to share this story with you.

One day a woman called the salon, distraught because her regular hairdresser had ruined her hair. The woman came in immediately for a consultation.

When she arrived and sat down in the chair, her hair was perfect. Her bob was well cut, her highlights were lovely.

The stylist asked her who her regular hairdresser was. The salon community is fairly small, and this hairdresser was well known and had a long, respectable career.

My co-worker told the woman that her hair was perfect and that she knew the man who had done the work and had nothing but respect for him. She commented that whatever the woman's problem was, it had nothing to do with her hair.

The woman became hysterical and wailed, "I'm turning 50!"

You may have heard this before, but a hairdresser is "a beautician, not a magician." If you are all twisted up inside, nothing we do to you outside is going to fix it.

My co-worker sent the client out of the salon with instructions to go back to her hairdresser and apologize for being insane.

I saw a tiny taste of this myself recently.

A client I have known for years is turning 40. She is a college professor and has a toddler and before she turns 40, she wants to "look cute."

I can cut her hair, and I can color it. I can even re-color it if it isn't EXACTLY perfect. But "cute" is an attitude, not a haircut.

People constantly bring in pictures of celebrities whose hair they would like. The top vote getter of all time is Meg Ryan. But it isn't her haircut that these clients really want. It's her "cute". Meg Ryan is cute. It comes from inside her. Her hair is just an outward representation of what is inside her.

When I was in high school, I had a friend who was cute. She was a cheerleader, her birthday cake had Smurfette on it, even my dad thought she was cute.

I wanted to be cute.

I was average. I wasn't unattractive, but I wasn't stunning. I had glasses and braces. I did have bigger boobs than many of my friends, but I sure as hell wasn't cute!

I am actually cuter now than I was then. I have run into people who haven't seen me in a decade and they comment on how young and cute I look.

I am sure it has something to do with the fact that I actually am happy and enjoy my life more than I did then. That, and the bangs.

Stress and unhappiness can make you look and feel old and unattractive.

Recent research actually shows that stress causes the individual cells in your body to age more rapidly.

Screw that!

Are you really willing to let stress make you look and feel old? I am much too vain to let that happen.

If inner peace can bring outer beauty, sign me up!

There is also something to be said for making peace with the body you have. Being OK in your own skin translates into confidence, and confidence is attractive!

Just don't cross the line from confidence to cockiness.

Confidence is attractive.

Cockiness is not.

People treat you a certain way based on how they perceive you (and how you perceive yourself.)

I lived in a small town in high school, so there weren't a lot of boys to go around.

It happened that my cute friend and I would occasionally have a date with the same boy. She would talk to me about her dates after the fact, as teenage girls do, and I would hear the stories of how the boy was the perfect gentleman. They went to dinner or they went to a movie, and he brought her home and gave her a little kiss.

I would then go out with the same boy and I would spend 3 or 4 hours trying to keep his amazing octopus-like hands out of my clothes!

I was lamenting this fact to a male friend one day who spelled it out for me. "When guys look at her, they want to spoil her and take care of her. When guys look at you, they want to take your clothes off."

Well, Hell! Must have been the boobs.

Have a little fun!

I bought my first car when I was 25.

Before that I drove my parents', my grandparent's, and my boyfriend's cars. And I rode the bus.

My first car was a small compact 4 door sedan. Next one was a well-used, more luxurious sedan. Then I got a little convertible Volkswagen Cabrio. That was fun! But I learned there are some downsides to convertibles.

For instance, sunglasses are not enough to protect you from the bright light. Since there is no top to the car, the light comes at you from above the glasses. So I had to wear a hat with a brim. I found a ball cap worked best, because it also kept my hair out of my face and stayed on in the wind.

The other thing is that when you are moving, the temperature is moderated by the wind, but when you stop at a traffic light, it can get really hot!

The final nail in the coffin of my convertible ownership was the fact that I had no garage available and one night while it was parked outside, some creep sliced the top with a knife.

I sold it shortly thereafter and got another practical car. By now I had the dogs and so I got an SUV so I could haul them about. But that giant thing just never felt right.

I got rid of it when I moved my salon downtown and had to park in an old building where space was tight.

I now drive a MINI Cooper. And let me tell you, it is fun! There's something about it that just seems to make people smile. Maybe because it is small, maybe because there are still relatively few of them on the street and they are something of a novelty, maybe because the front grill makes it look like the car is smiling.

I stopped for a drive-through coffee and the girl I'd never seen before said "Oh my God, this car is perfect for you!"

I think she might be right.

What does happiness look like?

I have a friend whose nickname is Happy!

What a concept. And if you met her, you would know why. People are always glad to see her. When she walks into a room, people smile. I can't explain it. She just exudes happiness.

She worked for many years in the physical therapy section of a nursing home. Now if you have ever had physical therapy, you know it is not always a pleasant experience. So you can imagine that an aged, injured person might not look forward to their session.

But when they would see her, they would smile. Being around her was a good thing, and it made the therapy more pleasant.

I'm not saying her life doesn't, on occasion, suck. It does. But who she is never changes.

She is currently in the middle of a divorce. She decided it was appropriate after her husband fired her from her position as hostess at the restaurant they'd opened together. He said she was bad for business.

Even my teenage son thought that was a stupid thing to do, and he knows stupid! It's hard to imagine how a joyful, effervescent hostess could be bad for a restaurant. But what do I know?

I have spent many hours and many bottles of wine with this friend trying to figure out what happened and went wrong in this relationship. They went to counseling before they got married, so she knew there were some issues.

She has come to realize that she probably should not have married him in the first place.

But she was getting older and she really wanted a baby.

She forgot to mention that she wanted a happy marriage AND a baby.

Oops.

What are you afraid of?

Fear is the most horribly misunderstood human emotion.

The basic biological imperative for fear is to keep us from blindly killing ourselves. If you are afraid that you might get hit by a car if you try to walk across the freeway, you will be less likely to try to walk across the freeway and therefore more likely to live.

So why does fear disable so many people from living a full life? Why do we allow our fears to keep us bottled up into tiny lives instead of living big, bold, blazing lives?

Richard Branson (CEO of the Virgin companies, adventurer and philanthropist) seems to be a person who has figured this out.

Don't get me wrong. A little fear is a good thing. A lot of fear is just plain stupid.

When I was in my 20's, I took the train from Seattle to San Antonio, making a handful of stops along the way to visit my parents and friends. The friend I was meeting in San Antonio was afraid to come to the train station to pick me up.

I took the train, all by myself, over 3000 miles and many days. She couldn't drive her own car in her own city. That just sucks. I took a cab to her apartment, and I have to say that my view of her changed after that.

I had an opinion of this girl based on years of knowing her in high school. And after this one incident, I looked at her differently. I judged her fear as a weakness.

Now maybe her fear was entirely justified for her, and maybe it was wrong of me to judge her. But I felt sorry for her. I thought it was sad that there were things that seemed perfectly reasonable to me that frightened her.

I am certainly not the bravest soul you'll ever meet. I was rather cautious as a child. It was my brother who talked me into jumping off the roof and taking rides in the dryer. It was sure hard to take the first step, but it was sure fun once I took it.

But everything is relative. I am sure there are some things that would frighten me that Richard Branson would thoroughly enjoy!

Perception colors reality.

I had a chance to learn this lesson in one brilliant flash.

Early in my relationship with my husband, I was at his apartment while he had guests. They were friends that he had known for years and I was definitely the new kid on the block.

I distanced myself from them while they had a grand time, having drinks and chatting animatedly.

I got annoyed.

I probably felt left out. (When you are in a new relationship, you have a tendency to want to monopolize your partner's time and attention.)

The more I thought about it, the more irritated I got.

After an hour or so, I looked at my new beau and was startled to see that I did not think he was attractive. I was startled because an hour before that, I thought he was darn cute.

So what had changed, I pondered?

I thought about my feelings and I wondered if I could find him attractive again. This was disturbing, because I had recently decided I loved him and it would suck to find myself in love with someone I didn't find attractive.

So I devised an experiment. I took a deep breath and closed my eyes. I thought about all the traits I found attractive in him.

I remembered moments that were joyful and pleasant.

I let my heart be filled with love for him.

And then I opened my eyes and smiled.

There was my guy, smiling at me, with kindness and love in his eyes.

And he looked better than he had a few minutes ago.

I guess that when you look at people with love in your heart, you find them more pleasing to look at.

Next time you think your partner is unattractive, try changing your perspective.

Maybe what's wrong with them – is you.

I especially liked this new perspective because it gave me some insight in to a relationship I had in the past. He often told me I was unattractive.

I would look in the mirror and wonder, "Am I pretty?"

He certainly didn't think so.

Maybe he wasn't looking at me with love in his heart.

Why did I let his opinion of me get under my skin?

What you think of me is none of my business.

Boy, was I a "pleaser."

I really needed people to like me, so I would do whatever I could think of to try to make it happen.

I found it didn't work out quite as well or as often as I thought it should.

I would bend over backwards and some people still wouldn't like me.

I had been told often enough what my "flaws" were.

I was loud.

I was opinionated.

I was flashy.

So clearly, I was unlovable.

Well, mention that to a counselor and see what they have to say!

"Does your self-worth rely on the opinion of others?"

"Are opinions facts?"

I left that session with an assignment and a mantra.

I wore a little buzzer on my hip that vibrated every 10 minutes or so. Every time it went off, I was supposed to say to myself, "I am loved and lovable."

Sounds pretty silly, right?

But isn't feeling unlovable even sillier?

I finally got that message and used that little gizmo to remind myself of some other truths.

You write the script of your life.

Maybe you should put some effort into writing it in a way that will bring you closer to happiness.

I had a boyfriend the summer before my sophomore year in high school. He broke up with me the first day of school.

I had a tough time getting over it. Over the next three years, we would occasionally date each other, but mostly he played hard to get by dating other people and moving on with his life.

I wouldn't let it go.

I really believed that this was The Man for me.

I wrote sappy poetry.

I asked his friends about him.

I left notes in his locker.

I drove by his house.

I think today they call it "stalking".

I moved away after high school and you would think that 3000 miles would be enough distance for me to get over him.

Noooooo!

It took me years. Years! What kind of madness is that?

He had married and had children and I was in a relationship, and I still pined for him.

What a waste of time!

I decided it was time to put this phantom behind me, so I wrote a story in which I spurned him.

I turned the tables.

I even had the character that represented him end up old and alone!

And then I was done.

I stopped thinking about him and moved on with my life.

Better late than never!

Try it yourself.

If you have something from your past that you are spending too much energy dwelling over, write a story and have it turn out differently.

For that matter, try it for something in the future!

Write out how you would like your life to unfold.

Put some serious thought into it.

Really consult your heart.

Maybe you can put yourself in a frame of mind that will help you accomplish your goals and put you on the path to happiness.

You matter.

I knew Joyce for a handful of years before she had cancer.

She was my mother's age, but I really felt a connection with her. You know how some people just "get" you? Joyce was one of those people.

We had a great time over the years being sarcastic together and laughing and bitching about her workplace (she worked in Community Mental Health and if you can't laugh about that, you'll go crazy!)

My personality is more Texas-high-school-football-coach / stand-up-comic than it is warm and fuzzy, so when really bad things happen, people expect that I will do what needs to be done and do it with humor.

One day Joyce told me that there were no more treatment options and that this was going to be her last visit to the salon because she probably wouldn't be alive in 6 weeks and if she was, she would be so doped up on morphine that she wouldn't care about her hair.

I laughed with her and then I went into the back room to mix up her color formula.

I closed the door behind me, fell to the floor and fell apart.

I cried for a good five minutes.

Then I wiped my eyes, took a deep breath and with a smile on my face, went back to apply her color. She didn't need tears from me. She had plenty of them with and from her family. What she needed from me was one last chance to feel like a normal, healthy person.

I went to her funeral, and I felt a little awkward because I didn't know her friends and family except through stories she told about them while I was doing her hair.

As the afternoon wore on, I would occasionally chat with the person nearest me and they would ask how I knew her.

I told them I did her hair and the greatest thing happened: Every one of the people I spoke to told me that Joyce had told them how much she loved going to get her hair done, and what a great time she had at the salon, and what a smart-ass her hairdresser was.

A hairdresser may have a thousand clients, but a client has one hairdresser.

What I learned from Joyce is that life is unpredictable.

What I learned from her funeral is that what I do for a living makes a difference in peoples lives.

Everything in your past has made you the person you are today.

Once upon a time I was an education major. It was one of the many majors I was trying on in my two years at community college. I started with musical theater, but while I can act and I can sing, I can not dance.

I have tried.

It is not pretty.

I tried journalism for a while. I like to write and I love to edit other people's writing. But the hours sucked!

There are deadlines to meet and you often have to give up sleep to meet them. Yuk.

I actually left community college (after more than two years) without a degree.

I just couldn't figure out what I wanted to do.

I ended up as a hairdresser because I had an uncle in the business and it looked like he had a good time at his job and made a decent living.

And I didn't know what the hell else to do with my life.

Believe it or not I am actually using all of the things I learned in college. (Which is better than some people can say. I know a woman with a Masters in Botany who, last I heard worked for the phone company.)

When I present my seminars, I use my theater skills and my education skills.

Journalism taught me to clear away what is unnecessary.

That helps in writing and in life!

So who am I?

If you really want to get me riled up, bring up the topic of public education. I have tons of opinions on what is happening and very few of them are positive.

I have been bitching about it for some time, but nothing seems to be changing!

(Hmmm, could that mean that pissing and moaning about something doesn't actually change it?)

I have come to realize that if education is big priority in my life, then I need to take a lesson from Bill Gates and put my money where my mouth is.

So I have decided to do something.

A portion of the sales of this book will go to education.

Annie Wright is a small private school in my city. (www.aw.org)

When I was a little girl, I desperately wanted to go there.

We were (by no means) a family of means, and so I did not attend.

Thanks to the incredible generosity of her grandparents, my daughter attends there.

I have decided that paying for even one kid to get a good start is better than bitching about the problems of education as a whole.

It is better to light one candle than to curse the darkness.

I have also thought about running for a seat on the local school board, but I watched a brilliant, highly educated, interesting, passionate, qualified friend of mine do that and she didn't get elected.

And elections are expensive! Those damn yard signs alone are costly.

Perhaps when I have am older and less abrasive in my opinions, I will give it a try.

What is important to you?

One time-tested method for getting some perspective on life is to give of yourself to something you believe in.

You can give your money (it is always appreciated) but you will get more out giving if you give of yourself.

Volunteer opportunities are endless, and I guarantee it is hard to feel sorry for yourself when you are helping someone else.

I had a client who was a student at a private high school and was whining to me that his school had instituted a new policy. They required 40 hours of community service in order to graduate. Let me help you with the math. You have four years of high school to accomplish this. We're talking 10 hours a year!

I told him to quit acting like a spoiled, selfish brat and to look at this as an opportunity to give instead of take for the first time in his life.

I am a big fan of youth service programs. Our kids are often so self-absorbed that they have no concept that there are people in their very community whose lives are filled with struggle. Seeing the real world can go a long way in making adjustments to wretched attitudes.

Will this help me be happy?

We are all faced with choices in life.

Sometimes decisions are hard.

You can ask yourself which path will bring you closer to true happiness, and that might clear away some of the confusion.

Remember that every one of us deserves happiness.

Remember that you can give of yourself without giving up yourself.

Remember that sometimes you have to compromise.

Remember that there is always someone with a sadder tale than yours.

Remember that happiness is a choice you make every day.

If you really can't make a choice, you can try these ideas:

What would Jesus do?

What would Elvis do?

What would Joan Jett do?

That should help inject a little humor in your situation and you may see it in a different light.

Don't stand in the way of you own happiness and don't put it off.

Beauty advice from a true beauty.

I have read this numerous times and I assume it to be a true quote from Audrey Hepburn.

She was a beautiful young woman, but her actions made her a beautiful person.

For attractive lips, speak words of kindness.

For lovely eyes, seek out the good in people.

For a slim figure, share your food with the hungry.

For beautiful hair, let a child run his fingers through it once a day.

For poise, walk with the knowledge that you never walk alone.

What a woman should have and know.

I received this email this AM. I think it wraps up this exercise nicely.

EVERY WOMAN SHOULD HAVE a set of screwdrivers, a cordless drill, and a black lace bra.

EVERY WOMAN SHOULD HAVE one friend who always makes her laugh, and one who lets her cry.

EVERY WOMAN SHOULD HAVE at least one good piece of furniture not previously owned by anyone else in her family.

EVERY WOMAN SHOULD HAVE eight matching plates, wine glasses with stems, and a recipe for a meal that will make her guests feel honored.

EVERY WOMAN SHOULD HAVE a feeling of control over her destiny.

EVERY WOMAN SHOULD KNOW how to fall in love without losing herself.

EVERY WOMAN SHOULD KNOW how to quit a job, break up with a lover, and confront a friend without ruining the friendship.

EVERY WOMAN SHOULD KNOW when to try harder and when to walk away.

EVERY WOMAN SHOULD KNOW that she can't change the length of her calves, the width of her hips, or the nature of her parents.

EVERY WOMAN SHOULD KNOW that her childhood may not have been perfect, but it is over.

EVERY WOMAN SHOULD KNOW what she would and wouldn't do for love or money.

EVERY WOMAN SHOULD KNOW how to live alone even if she doesn't like it.

EVERY WOMAN SHOULD KNOW whom she can trust, whom she can't, and why she shouldn't take it personally.

EVERY WOMAN SHOULD KNOW where to go, be it to her best friend's kitchen table or a charming inn in the woods, when her soul needs soothing.

EVERY WOMAN SHOULD KNOW what she can and can't accomplish in a day, a month and a year.

Real help if you need it.

If you are one of the people who truly need help, please get it!

Every day you spend in the darkness is a day of happiness you are missing out on.

Every community has a mental health hotline that can direct you to assistance and your doctor is ready and willing to help you if you just speak up.

There is no shame in seeking help.

Getting help is not selfish!

If you ever think that people would be better off without you, then you need help.

You owe it to your family to take care of yourself.

I promise you, you can be happy!